Contradictions

Sophie J. Morgan

BookLand press

Published by BookLand Press
15 Allstate Parkway, Suite 600
Markham, Ontario L3R 5B4
www.booklandpress.com

Printed and bound in Canada

Front cover image © Jakub Gojda

Library and Archives Canada Cataloguing in Publication

Morgan, Sophie J., author
Contradictions / Sophie J. Morgan.

Poems.
Issued in print and electronic formats.
ISBN 978-1-77231-017-7 (pbk.).--ISBN 978-1-77231-018-4 (epub).--
ISBN 978-1-77231-019-1 (pdf)

I. Title.

PS8626.O7465C65 2015 C811'.6 C2015-902422-6
C2015-902423-4

Canada Council for the Arts / Conseil des arts du Canada

ONTARIO ARTS COUNCIL
CONSEIL DES ARTS DE L'ONTARIO
an Ontario government agency
un organisme du gouvernement de l'Ontario

We acknowledge the support of the Canada Council for the Arts, which last year invested $157 million to bring the arts to Canadians throughout the country. We acknowledge the support of the Ontario Arts Council (OAC), an agency of the Government of Ontario. We acknowledge the financial support of the Ontario Media Development Corporation for our publishing activities.

Table of Contents

Illusion

Thoughts that are as clear
as a mirage in a dream
that emerge from thin air
and are difficult to see
they are far away from reach
further away from comprehension
they appear and disappear
without a single trace
the illusion that appears
behind this mirage
strikes
bright and clear as a lightning bolt
revealing the secrets
behind the illusion
behind the ambivalence
with great prominence and beauty
to those who stood by their mirage
wandered in their dreams
and waited
ever so patiently
for the lightning to strike
for their thoughts
for the mirage in their dreams

Rooted Within

Like a system of roots
beneath the ground
our choices
our lives
our adventures
are all intertwining with one another
overlapping
combining
growing
with some stronger
and some thinner than others
some leading to healthy lives
and others leading to the ones that were left behind
the intricate relationship
between the roots and the lives that they lead to
is so exceptional
so hidden to the world
yet so apparent in our lives
constantly evolving
changing
guiding us
that the result
is only realized
when the lives are at stake

Fragments of Reality

Lost in the melody
wandering amidst the sound
off in another world
but knowing
exactly where to go
along with the tune
until disrupted by a thought
a fragment of reality
and not only losing the harmony
but becoming lost forever
until the song
is resurrected again

Paradox

I never strike it out so much
that I can't see
I never ignore it so much
that I can't remember
I never love so much
that I become infatuated
I've never lost so much
that I lose myself

Waves of Time

Imprinted forever
with a stamp
and a dye
leaving a lasting impression
for the next world to see
but as the waves of time
continue to crash
on the shores of our lives
the stamp
that was once there
coloured with the most prominent dye
faded
and washed away with time

Tranquility of a Blank Canvas

Each blank canvas
will be started with a single stroke
enhanced by colours
and completed by emotions
for every masterpiece
there is a genius behind it all
for every gallery
a curator who speaks the truth
and for every stroke
a person who saw through the haze
until the very end

Prosperous Minds

Thoughts
worth more than a penny
ideas
that turn on a dime
dreams
that are worth the catcher
and moments
that transcend time
all lead to
the greatest pile of riches
the wildest of dreams
and a life
that never ends

The Perfect Moment

The sun
came out
and shone brightly
the clouds
disappeared
revealing a sapphire blue sky
the waters were calm
without a single ripple or wave
the wind
blew away
taking all worries and doubts
along with it
just for this moment
a moment of serenity

Misconceptions

Fierce
aggressive
yet kind
sweet
and calm
this misconception
is beyond belief
the truth and lies
right and wrong
reality and stereotypes
all becoming twisted and changed
different in everyone's eyes
like a circus mirror
we all have our own truths
and this is mine

Newfound Clarity

Lost in a new thought
remembering
all the battles that were fought
feeling
the cool wind blow away
along with all of the words that I refused to say
but choosing to go ahead
I dismiss
the words that were never said
look down
to peer at my own reflection
now knowing
of this untouched direction
standing beneath nothing
but a clear blue sky
I see a butterfly
flutter in the corner of my eye
and with this newfound clarity
I am finally able
to reach my prosperity

Silent Observer

Looking
upon the world
understanding that it will never be mine
never to experience
or to behold
I am simply an observer
a prisoner behind bars
watching the wonders of the world
pass me by

In Disguise

Unsure of which mask
will fit on this new face
but too afraid to ask
or to find a new place
choosing a new disguise
and wishing to be set free
discarding all the lies
as I drift off to the endless sea
wandering in an everlasting maze
and choosing to take a final chance
I exit this phase
and escape with this trance
I open my eyes
to recognize that nothing has gone amiss
and after countless masks and futile tries
I am finally in a state of pure bliss

Reflection

Wandering off
into the land of mirrors
standing above my reflection
above who I am
above the world beneath my feet

Sincere Solace

Looking upon
those who roam
from behind smoked glass
peering out
without anyone looking in
no questions
comments
stares
or remarks
behind the glass
watching
as thoughts dissolve
and dissipate
like clouds in the sky
and pondering
upon the thought
of sincere solace

Speechless Conversations

Roaming
looking about
upon the world
and listening to
speechless conversations
replaced with loud thoughts
silent voices
and muted remarks
only audible
to those of the same kind
with the same minds
cut from the same cloth
and sewn with the same thread
and the rest
are left behind
deaf to these words
but familiar
with their own silent voices

When the Night Falls

The bright moon
casts a shadow
of the black woods
with its soft light
against the harsh ground
when the night falls
the lights are turned off
the masks are put away
the costumes disappear
raindrops fall to hit the ground
along with remnants of reality
nothing is left
but the silence
of the harsh truth
the certainty
that what lies in the dark woods
is not unknown

Sewn Together

A loom
weaving in and out
over and under
again and again
while the progress seems so minute
the piece is growing
with every weave
with every strand
with every choice
using a spool
and a thread
sewing together
the pieces of the puzzle
that have been undiscovered
never completed
stitch by stitch
thread by thread
as the answer
is sewn together

Smouldering Perceptions

A wildfire
from within
spreading from the core
destroying false realities
creating smouldering perceptions
destructively forcing its way through
only to be extinguished
by the cold truth
leaving behind
the ashes
of what once was
to be scattered
blown away by the wind
off into the air
along with the thick, grey smoke
heavy with the weight
of all of our dreams
drifting away
to a new land

After the Show

On the outside
bright lights
and colours are displayed
putting on a show
for all to see
but as time passes on
the show comes to an end
the curtain falls
and the bright lights
that once caught all the attention
disappear
and fade away
into the shadows
as the next show comes on

Within the Eyes of the World

Searching for answers
along the horizon
searching for truth
for the answers of reality
within the eyes of the world
searching for the light
the radiance
that will transform it all
only to realize
that I've been searching
all along
for the sun
behind the wrong clouds

Flawless Transformation

Turning the key
of a long-locked door
to open it
and to find nothing inside
simply an empty, desolate room
with a window that was once a door
and a door that was once a wall
expecting to be speechless
and to discover greatness
but instead
finding perfection

A Day in Autumn

The bold colours of autumn
presented to the world
fall to the ground
like droplets of rain
cast beauty over all
as the leaves swiftly fall
blown away by the wind
falling on the road
on the rooftops
in the rivers
the leaves float away
away from each other
becoming separated
from their roots
from their tree
from their forest
joining the stream
that flows on
without an end

Endless Journey

How long was I lost
away
travelling in my own mind
on the ship of my thoughts
afloat on my imagination
drifting on a single hope
paddling with my aspirations
against the currents of factuality
and against the winds of time?
I am steadily paddling
then slowly, I am guided
back to the shores of reality
and discover the truth behind it all

Leaving One Behind

Finding the rope
tying the knot
tightening it with hope
and loosening it with thought
no knots left untied
leaving everything behind
with nothing left to hide
only hope and thoughts to bind
choosing one above all
and with a future to create
one takes a fall
and one becomes fate

Midnight Revelation

Observing the night sky
watching the shooting stars pass by
noticing the crescent moon shine
looking down and seeing two branches intertwine
and further down below
the flowers continue to grow
as I fall back looking at the starry sky
I begin to realize
that it wasn't a dream
it's all exactly what it seems

Irreversible Differences

A gaze can change the world
striking a new thought
like a match
between the new and the old
the before and the after
of the mind
of the person
of the gaze that changed the world

Stargazing Epiphany

A sudden burst
a spark in the sky
faster than a bolt of lightning
strong enough
to take away
all of the city lights
revealing the infinite stars
of the night sky
and leaving behind
nothing
to those who ignore it
but everything
to those who have been waiting
for an eternity
to see the stars
that were always there

Forgotten Moments

Leaving everything undone
forgetting about it all
everything behind
everything in the past
and becoming undone
just like what was forgotten

Daydreaming

Wind, wind here and there
oh, it's blowing everywhere
it's pouring and raining
and time is only gaining
I wait and I wait as the hours pass by
and just stare at this horrendous and stormy grey sky
I am still sitting alone
contemplating the unknown
but when I do this
not a thought goes amiss
this is called the perfect time to think
as it creates a link
between the body and mind
during this time you never know what you may find

Everlasting Questions

Who made all these choices?
who hears all these voices?
is any of it true?
or is it all just one big skew?
how will we ever know wrong from right?
how will we ever know day from night?
we have no proof
for all we know this could be one big spoof
we have no guarantee
all we can do is wait and see

Desolation

Entering a land that is so sparse
coming from a land that is so dense
not a person here
like there used to be over there
feeling so lost
and wanting to be found
feeling too much emptiness
longing for a land that is complete
wanting to see light
but only seeing darkness
wanting to look up at the sky
but only seeing the ground

Two Worlds

In one day I can enter two different worlds
I step outside
it is scorching and immensely hot
one step inside and it is brutally cold
but when I stand in between
trying to balance it
one world takes over
there are no options
between these two worlds
one is cold and unforgiving but offers rewards
another is free and lively but offers consequences
my mind spins as I choose
I wonder what would happen if both worlds collide
they can't and the coldness takes over
until it is destroyed

Purity

This is lost from the world
no one is pure
the way we were meant to be
even in solidarity
we are never untainted
the only chance we ever had to be unique
was snatched away from us
involuntarily, without permission
alone we think we are ourselves
innocent, kind, different
everywhere else
we attempt to be ourselves
we are tainted
I'm not pure because of someone else
someone else isn't pure because of me
we never did anything wrong, at least not all of us
but it's not life, events, actions, or thoughts
that obliterated whatever purity we had
no, it's us
every single one of us taking truths
and trying to salvage whatever is left to prove
that we are the anomalies
who make the world special

Truth or Lie?

Who am I to others?
how do I know if the world I have placed myself in
is the truth?
it could all be a lie
but if it were
wouldn't I feel something?
or am I living in an ignorant state of bliss?

Elemental World

I'm inside of my virtual world
this world is a difficult one to live in
and strategic planning is required
one cannot simply enter this world without a clue
one will be destroyed in a matter of seconds
and elementals will blame you
this is my world
and only some others will understand
the world of planning and creations
is known to us like the back of our hand

Time Never Stops

Clocks and hands moving back and forth
constantly
time never stops
is my time the same as yours?
is it the same as anyone's?
time can separate us from anything
it can isolate us
we are moving at a different speed
momentum
pace from everyone else
time is needed to perfect this error
but for now
we all live in our own worlds
with seconds and minutes constantly passing
alone and in segregation

Transcendence

Everything is blurry and misty
I see nothing
I wonder what is real
and what is fake
I am losing
but I am certain that someone else out there is winning
as I am walking around blindly
someone else can see clearly
losing isn't something I want
but it's sometimes what I need
and what I need is to learn
instead of being taught
taught how to find my way
through the pernicious mist

See and Feel

A lost mind
a special mind
trying to find its way home
through thoughts and feelings
not what it sees
but what it feels
each breath a belief
each blink a vision
of the world
where anyone can tell me what they see
but can you tell me how you feel?
in words?
on paper?

Our Thoughts

There's no such thing as your own thought
someone else is guaranteed
to have the same thought as you
we all share our thoughts
often I have thoughts inside my head
they wander around freely like bubbles
floating in the air after being blown
but in a second
they disappear
lost forever
drifting off
into another mind

Chasing Dreams

Whenever I try to change something
make myself believe or trust
my head begins to ring
and my brain turns to rust
I look inside trying to find some truth
and when I do
I find some sort of contradiction
I think to myself
I must
but it's just another thought that I'd waste
trying to chase my dreams

Waiting for the Truth

I sit and I wait
ever so patiently
my mind is racing
and my heart is pounding
yet I have a blank expression on my face
I'm still waiting
but not for a person
not for a thing
but I'm waiting for the truth
despite this noun
it's not a thing
and I want it
more than anything
I have ever desired

Ideas in Turmoil

Inside the heart
the depths of this place
signals are racing
back and forth
constantly and neverending
one bad idea and it can go awry
turmoil can arise
not only for the mysterious and uncharted place
but also for its surroundings
this goes to show
that something is bound to go wrong
simply because not all ideas will conquer
it's a shame but it's the true fact
of what sustains humanity
and unfortunately us all

The Choice

I have the choice
suffocate in a dense haze
or survive in clear breaths
the switch is instantaneous and simple
just move the barrier
and choose
between the easy life
that each one of us takes for granted
or the difficult life we choose to avoid
for the sights of cold reality

Stigma

Who comes up with things?
who describes and defines them?
there really are no definitions
people simply make them up
are we being fooled?
there is no real proof
and we only rely on other humans for the answer
should we search for more?
or stop
thinking we have and know everything?

Mind Pendulum

Moving, swinging back and forth
come to me
stay with me
give me a reason
I see it swinging away from me
then coming back
I need you but I don't want you
or do I want you but I don't need you?
I see it swinging back away
but I know it will return again
it's both pleasure and pain
I need it but I don't want it
I don't want the pain
but I need the truth
both are priceless but
one holds more respect and desire than the other

Oblivion

Lying face down
my eyes are closed
everything is calm
as I slowly drift away
I suddenly fall into an abyss
not knowing where I am, what I hear, or what I see
I look back
then I look forward
I don't see the same
when I look back
I am surrounded by the safety of angels
when I look forward
I am surrounded and haunted by demons
in-between I feel so lost
but something very valuable has been found
under a heap of lies
I have found a very important truth

Whispers in the Wind

I listen
listen with depth and thought
it sounds strange but simultaneously intriguing
all I hear is the bitter wind with faint and soulful cries
like the dead are whispering to me
asking for help
desperate to escape
the wind turning into cold, bone chilling howls
their words changing into shrieks as they try to escape
but they are trapped
I am useless to them
no way in
no way out
lost inside forever

Phenomena

A house with no door
a maze with no exit
a day with no light
a world with no people
a clock with no hands
time seems to go on forever
and I don't know when it will ever end

Nothing Appears the Same

Before I leave
and when I arrive
there is a difference
my eyes don't see the same
before, I could see nothing
now, I am aware of everything
every generalization
turns into specific details
nothing is the same
but nothing is different
my old soul has died
but my new one has been born
changing me forever

Contradictions

What can harm us
can make us the happiest people alive
I often think of things in two ways
negative and positive
quite obvious, I know
the negatives turn into phobias and exclusion
towards yourself and the experience
the positives calm you down
and invite you to the journey and the destination
we don't control the way we think
we really don't
it's just our brain
but who says you can't outsmart yourself?
I believe the answer is no one
so, go ahead
trick yourself if you dare
sometimes it's for the better

Becoming of a Choice

Everything we have, see, and touch
is the becoming of a choice
it was someone's choice
to follow their dream
pursue their dream of developing something
chase their dream of creating something
go after their dream of being different
making something new
a new change in the world
everything is the becoming of a choice

Mirage

I have a pen in hand
and a spotless blank sheet of paper in front of me
immediately I start drawing
I refuse to look until I am done
all I know is that I am drawing
the sky, moon, stars, flowers
and whatever else my mind and hand
can produce in unison
finally, I have finished
I stand and pick up my piece
then I see
that I have a spotless, blank sheet of paper
in front of me
and I have never been more proud

Game of Chance

I have hundreds of coins
maybe even thousands
they flip and turn constantly
for the game of chance
will I be lucky?
I wait and I wait
for one lucky coin to land
one out of hundreds of other coins

Serenity

Casually drifting
floating in serenity and peace
gradually escaping reality
I slowly open my eyes
I find myself squinting
the light is too bright
all I see is clear, perfect blue
I am relaxed
but slightly scared
because I am clueless
lost and confused
I completely open my eyes
stand up
and find myself
only a few steps away from where I started

Days in Paradise

Set me free
let me go
take me somewhere new
do not lie
I will trust
every part of you
let's escape
let's get lost
learn things we never knew
let's go
run away
let's make all our dreams come true

Eternal Thoughts

Whenever I write something
I leave it
then I look at it again after a while
I am tempted to erase all of my work
start all over
from scratch
but then I stop myself
why?
because I will never erase my own thoughts
erasing my own thoughts would be a sin against
my brain
my mind
my soul
my spirit
my entire self
I could never erase a part of me
whether it be
past
present
or future
and I would never do it to anyone else
but eventually I may hoard
but I will not hoard pieces of paper
but my thoughts instead
as the years go by and as I live my life
going through all the milestones
I have yet to experience
I will be hoarding everything
all in my mind
and wishing to never let them go

Days Ahead

My biggest day is still unknown
even though I think I know it all
I believe I've done it all
my biggest dreams
worst nightmares
most genuine smiles
most sorrowful tears
the best day of my life
and even the worst
they aren't even here yet